UNTOLD STALKING STORY

By

Evelyn White

Authors Choice Press
New York   Bloomington

Untold Stalking Story

*Authors Choice Press
an imprint of iUniverse*

iUniverse books may be ordered through booksellers or by contacting:

*iUniverse
1663 Liberty Drive
Bloomington, IN 47403
www.iuniverse.com
1-800-Authors (1-800-288-4677)*

ISBN: 978-1-4401-8749-0 (pbk)

Printed in the United States of America

iUniverse rev. date: 10/29/09

PREFACE

Once there was black family living in the Delta of Mississippi. She was the seventh child born to a family of five sisters and eleven brothers. Our lives had the joy from learning to working together as a family.

My father was a Baptist minister, and he was a strong disciplinarian. As the leader, my mother worked with him to fulfill the obligations of family daily living. She tried to work with him to keep us together as a family unit. Their lives were not easy because survival meant many sacrifices, especially to maintain an economical standard of living in the Delta.

The community bonded together to make a living. We raised several crops. One in particular was cotton, and cotton was king. My father was a role model in the community, so he hired people to help pick cotton on our farm. I was very young, and I was the baby-sitter on the farm at an early age. As I grew, I became a farm hand, and I learned to do farm work, such as picking cotton, and vegetables, as well as a leader to chop and pick cotton.

Mississippi Delta was one of the most suitable land areas to raise farm products. These were black sharecroppers, and they worked on our farm to make extra money for their families. I think people came from various communities to make extra money, and they helped farm the land.

This community was part owned and bought by blacks. It is called the Teoc community, since I became familiar with it. Some notable Civil Rights workers and leaders are being mention in this book because of their impact on education in the twentieth century.

INTRODUCTION

My life started in the Teoc community in Carroll County bordering Leflore County. We communicated with Leflore because the town of Greenwood bustled with business. This business community meant sharing wealth. My father often sold cotton, vegetables, and shopped in this small town. Our livelihood depended on the business community in Greenwood.

My father traded and bought goods from this small business town. After one exciting day of trading, he brought home a new truck. In addition, to help with farming, he bought a new tractor. He was a strict businessperson, and the crops were strong in the early days of our prosperous farm, but the market yielded less. Therefore, he made fewer profits, but we worked harder. Sometimes, we worked other plantations to earn money. He saw to it that we always had food. We were to spend money buying from the store. When going to the plantations, most of the time, we bought food for lunch, such as cinnamon rolls, bologna, and crackers.

The family still finds time to laugh about farming. My brothers, sisters, and I have fun talking about the bad as well as the good times. We joke about money, school and relationships. Our father led us to the sanctuary to read the Bible and prayed astounding prayers. He was heard miles away, and he sang religious hymns joyfully. We learned early to sing, to pray, and to read the Bible. He taught us to participate in some religious activities. For example, he encouraged baptism at an early age.

Daddy was a proponent our community of education as well, and encouraged schooling at an early age. He participated in selecting teachers for our one-room school. He strongly emphasized moral habits for the community.

My father was a great motivator, and he left an everlasting impression on my life. This meant staying in touch with family, work, friends, and participating in religious settings. He was a patriarch, and most of the time domineering, even in the community. He was sometimes outspoken, but he kept a low profile. His influence helped the family learn how to grow in many ways.

His leadership helped me to seek a career in education. His abilities inspired me to learn how coping trained the mind, and how it deters poor behavior. Also, you will never forget indefinitely.

My mother's influence was toward education as well. She taught me to read my first schoolbooks. We learned to read Bible verses, and memorize. The family learned to help each other. Our parents were the role models for family even though; they did not finish high school. The family exposure to community culture vitalized our gifts to be teachers, preachers, carpenters, mechanics, and leaders. This pattern has helped us to endure today's standard of living.

I want to thank my father, mother, brothers, sisters, nephews, nieces, in-laws, grandchildren Gabrielle and Kentrell, and especially my son, Arcell Jr. and daughter Kareda Chantel Jacob. This group will long endure the pain and suffering, but most of all happiness we continue to share forever. Kentrell and Gabrielle shall learn life has a meaningful purpose. The future promises happiness. In addition, happiness is learned, and it is not a gift. God will bless each of us to look to the future with an inspiring attitude. This attitude of life given by God is the greatest gift of all. Even though, my father, two brothers and a sister are deceased, the bond of love-wealth between us remains forever. We celebrate this bond by hosting reunions, birthdays, and family vacations together annually. Unfortunately, not everyone has been thanked, but thanks to all who have had an impact on my life. However, most of all, I want to thank God for His grace and mercy.

Chapter 1
EARLY CHILDHOOD

During World War II, a black child was born to a couple named Edgar and Dovie Brown-White. This child was born in September 1945 and on the fourth, as was her father. She was the seventh of sixteen children, both boys and girls. She learned at an early age to do homemaking for the younger children. She did this task, while others worked in the field on the Delta farm. Our farm was black entrepreneurship next to an area of white owned-land. This plantation hired blacks to sharecrop or work on it.

We witnessed the culture of blacks, such as baseball, picnics, and other religious activities, especially, church services every Sunday. This meant the so-called pastoral Sunday was held on the first and second of each month. There were revivals each year. We participated in the BTU, Bible studies, prayer meetings, business meetings, conventions, and the chosen Sunday to feed the pastor. During revival each year, those who joined the church were baptized in the community creek.

The Teoc community was composed of former plantation folks from early slavery. Some names were former plantation owner last names. There is still gossip about blacks named by white folks, such as McCain. The land some McCain is living rumored to be owned by the white race. The story goes that a piece of the land was for a black woman or family who bore white children. The land never intended for blacks. It was borrowed from whites for future generations. In recent years, some family members wanted a title or deed because of their interest in becoming independent. They have lived and worked the land for years. This setting went little noticed in the Teoc community, but conversations of interest pass from one generation to another.

My father purchased eighty-five acres from a white woman in my early years. I am the first child to live on the acquired black-owned land in the family. This tradition became inevitable. As you may know, many blacks never left the South after the Civil War. Many never had the opportunity to own land. The provisional government gave black people seven acres and a mule after the Civil War. The blacks lived as vagrants and continued to live in slavery conditions, but never obtained the land. This meant working without pay in exchange for commodities. Many white people feared blacks' power for change. Therefore, they sharecropped or worked the land for little profits. Voting was made harder for blacks, with the required poll tax, and interpretation of the Constitution. Therefore, schools were segregated with whites reading books, which were later sent to the black schools. Eventually, a change was made to build some schools for the blacks.

Our land was very attractive with rich Delta soil. For example, we raised watermelons, peanuts, peas, okra, beans, sweet potatoes, Irish potatoes, onions, peppers, cane and syrup, and fruits, such as plums, berries, cottons and soybeans. There were chickens, hogs, cattle, horses, mules, geese, ducks, Ginny birds, rabbits, squirrels, deer, snakes, trees, fish, nuts, and snow. Of course, we had fun making ice cream from snow when it snowiest sometimes. Another outing was learning how to catch and cook certain birds over the fireplace in the winter. Life entailed hauling water from several miles away on a slide to bathe, wash, and drink. The food was meat from the chickens, hogs, and wild game yearly. We mainly worked on the farm every day and sometimes on Sunday evenings, if necessary. If it rained, my father chose work to do indoors for us. For example, shelling peas, beans, bunch greens, or what he called the "a truck patch" to sell in the town. At times, we would chop cotton in spots that were not too wet or do the "truck patch" or some cash crop. There were times when farm chores were done early in the morning before school.

Our school in the community was lead by the people. The schoolhouse had about six rooms. It consisted of grades pre premier through six. The school had a leader-called "Professor." It had one teacher per grade. The professor's family lived in a single dwelling. The teachers shared a house called the teacher's home. These educators had at least an eighth-grade education. I completed the first six years at the John McCain Elementary School, located in the Teoc, Mississippi and community. This school was partitioned into six areas for six grades. It is part of Senator John McCain's family heritage. The teachers were from outside the community. When students became old enough and finished

Chapter 2
ELEMENTARY, HIGH SCHOOL
AND COLLEGE SCHOOL DAYS

My elementary school days started at the age of six, around 1950. We learned to read and write. I read to my mother the book required. I read aloud to her, and she would correct the words missed. My younger sister and I shared the same grade until the second or third. My teacher tested my reading skills in the third grade. I recall her writing the letters together for me to read. I read them aloud to her. Then, she decided to "skip" to another grade. I was "skipped" twice. I think that it was my age. I started school at the age six, but we were called "pre-premier" and "primer" before being promoted to the first grade. My sister was younger, so I was "skipped" because of age, maturity and academic skills. I was very good in reading, art, plays, math, and social skills as a student. I missed my younger sister in grade school. My father would come to school to check on us. He bought us "school clothes," and dressed us alike. He tried very hard to help us in school, also. He became frustrated with money as farming needs changed. He tried to help us make a living in many ways.

Our farm yielded profits in its early investments stage. As the years went by, and changes were made in farming, crops were less profitable for blacks. Daddy tried to get ahead by investing in more land and money. He borrowed money from the FHA in Carrollton, Mississippi. Then, the profits were first, and we were stuck with the balance. This meant the crops turned into profitable or non-profitable. If we yielded profitably or if we had a "good year," Daddy was ahead for the next season. If we were non-profitable, the balance carried to the next year or season to repay. This cycle continued on our farm. He hardly ever broke even, and the land continued in debt.

As we continued to become of age, some of us went to college after high school. Daddy sponsored us to the best of his ability. My older brothers and sisters had the opportunity to continue their education. Some of them went off to finish high school at area schools for blacks. Then, in 1955 or 1956, schools for blacks were built in Carrollton. This school was Marshall High School. This gave us an opportunity for higher education.

Therefore, it was the last group at the John McCain Elementary. It was closed in 1956. I attended Marshall High School from grades seven through twelve and graduated in 1963. I learned to do a lot of homemaking, especially tailoring. We were instructed in English, math, science, biology, gym, choir, social studies, shorthand and a little typing. Some students became good at shorthand. I learned how to do it, but never excelled. In addition, geometry was one of the required credits.

Our extracurricular activities were basketball, choir, and homemaking. The district sponsored boys' and girls' basketball. I was mainly a homemaker student. I learned to sew and cook in high school. My homemaker teacher sponsored clubs to promote enrichment for the students. In my later years, the community sponsored the 4-H Club for black boys and girls. During this period, there was a focus on agriculture.

As the years changed our agricultural lifestyle, many blacks went north to make a better living as area became less vital. There were fewer jobs for blacks. Life became more sophisticated, and we began to demand better living conditions. One scenario consisted of the Emmitt Till murder in 1955. This cause of action brought about a change between the blacks and whites within the community. This sensational trial was in our community. It was widely publicized, and it is still a wound today in every society.

Our schools changed because of Brown v. Board of Education, 1954. For example, President Eisenhower ordered Central High School of Little Rock, Arkansas, to integrate its facilities in 1955. This forced integration changed the face of the South in all aspects of life. It led to the integration of all public facilities. This desegregation plan led to "freedom of choice," after President Kennedy became president in 1960. Then, the country witnessed the Space Age advances. For example, around 1961, John Glen orbited the earth in space. Indeed, we witnessed many advances in education. The Peace Corps, Voting Rights Acts, and the Civil Rights Act became the "core" or "heart" of politics" led by the President Kennedy and Vice President Lyndon

B. Johnson administrations. Thus, their programs were the "New Frontier" and the "Great Society" respectively. The "Great Society" program was widely known for its "War on Poverty," and President Johnson, from Texas, a former schoolteacher himself.

This administration was the focus of attention in the media because of the Vietnam War, and the President Kennedy assassination in 1963 as well. Thus, this era witnessed a new generation of people interested in working with the media and the plight of minorities led by Rev. Dr. Martin Luther King, Jr. This is the period of my coming to college from high school. Our community college, Mississippi Valley State University, at the time Mississippi Vocational College. Fortunately and unfortunately, I witnessed the exploration, assassination, war, war on poverty, integration or desegregation, crime, and crime against race relations. During President Kennedy's term in office, I Witnessed colleges integrated, and the slaying of the three civil rights workers in Mississippi. We were working to have the right to vote. In addition, several churches were destroyed by fire. Our community church, Mitchell Spring Missionary Baptist Church, was burned down in the 1960s. In our community, we worked with civil rights workers from the north and west. We traveled together, and we worked at churches. My family entertained several white civil rights workers by feeding and sheltering them during the day. I was a college student, and I commuted daily to Mississippi Vocational College. I did lots of housework, such as cooking and cleaning. Our role was singing in the choir during the civil rights movement, and later voter poll watching. Our father did not want us to go out and work in the civil rights field to protest. He feared for our lives. We met some of the important civil rights notables, such as Dr. Martin L. King, Jr., on his visit to Greenwood, Mississippi, during the 1960s. I recall Marty and John Allen living with us during the day.

During this stage, I was able to earn a Bachelor of Science degree from Mississippi Valley State University in social science in 1966. I spent three years and the summer studying to earn the degree. During the second summer session, I needed a class in 1966 to complete my course work or degree plan, so a friend and I visited the Glen Allen's community for a job interview. This was my first teaching assignment, and it lasted until around 1974.

Then, I went on my first interview to teach, after a friend told me about positions open to blacks. These positions were open for teachers in elementary and secondary schools. The school was Glen Allen High School, Glen Allen, Mississippi. A white principal was seeking black teachers. He was Mr. Choate. He interviewed two of us. Her name was Dorothy Edward, and she became the English teacher. I was petite and offered a job in elementary education, but I was seeking a position in social science. I taught elementary one year, then taught social studies there for six years. While there, we were to integrate or "desegregate now." The high school was for a year at Riverside High School, at Avon, Mississippi. The issue was busing to achieve integration. This policy became very controversial in the South and North. It was controversial, but it was a means to desegregate the population.

President Kennedy and his brother, Bobby Kennedy, the Attorney General of the United States, was the threshold of leadership, setting the precedent to desegregate education, because of "separate and unequal facilities." Although, President Eisenhower enforced the Brown v Board of Education decision 1954 by using federal troops, the issue of race has not ceased and its problems still linger today. Attorneys and former U. S. Justice Thurgood Marshall has worked tirelessly on these cases. Our system continues to fall short in improving race relations, and social skills remain tarnished.

There were many dedicated individuals who worked to improve civil rights during this era, but few became famous. We will never know the names of many who made sacrifices in this arena. These notable individuals made an impact on our lives for quality education, and this is the reason a few are mentioned in this book. Our leaders implemented the law and policies to help all races to fulfill the dream, as well as to comply with democratic principles.

While teaching at Glen Allen High School, I attended Mississippi College at Clinton, Mississippi, during desegregation, and I received a master in education for social science in 1973. Glen Allen was a small community, but it was very progressive and lively. I enjoyed working there, and many of the students were very knowledgeable, intelligent, and outgoing. They worked hard to strive for the best in life, and they were energetic in learning to be the best educators. I was teaching black culture most of the time. I felt at home while there. Some of the students went to some of the most notable colleges and universities in Mississippi. There were recruiters for them with the Federal

Bureau of Investigation during the 1960s and 1970s. I had the opportunity to recommend several of my social studies students to this department. We were successful in sports, such as football and basketball, for a small school. The students worked hard at sports. I did further study in social studies at Mississippi State University and University of New York during the 1970s.

As we moved to Texas in 1979, I attended Lee College in Baytown, where I received three hours of credit, and became certified to teach social science in May 1980. I was to work in the Houston Independent School District as a special education resource teacher for four years. The school district required certification, so; I went to University of Houston in Clear Lake.

After several years as a classroom teacher, I became interested in supervision and the doctoral program. The doctoral program at Texas Southern University made some drastic changes during the time I applied in the fall of 2000. In the summer, 2002, I became an assistant principal with the alternative program in educational Administration. Later, I decided to seek a master's degree in education and graduated in the summer of 2005.

Chapter 3
TEACHING CAREER

As mentioned, my teaching career began with student teaching at John F. Kennedy High School in 1966 under the director of a social science teacher in Mound Bayou, Mississippi. My student teaching was a learning experience as designed to promote educators' endeavors to be the best teachers in the United States. My environment was normal, but I could not believe classmates' experiences as told by them at the end of our group session May 1966. For example, several experienced unusual student behavior, such as loud noise, inattentiveness, being off task, or being ignored completely in class when asked to respond in certain situations. They told of circumstances when shouting aloud was necessary, but inappropriate. I had to repeat on several occasions the appropriate behavior but nothing was serious for office visitations.

My next assignment was Lakeside High School in Lake Village, Arkansas. I wanted fewer rigorous' jobs because I had earned my Master's degree. Therefore, my assignment was teaching United States History to eleventh graders. I enjoyed working with them, and their extra-curricula activities, such as student councils, parades, sports, as well as some drama or plays. This assignment was interesting in that education became a milestone. We were to participate in several projects. One in particular was meeting in Hot Springs, Arkansas, during 1976 or 1977. Those meetings dealt with IDEA (reference to special education). We were participating in speaking engagements of renowned feminists from other parts of the country. The principal made all the assignments, and he drove us by bus, including the faculty at the high school, as well as overnight stays. In addition, there were other participants from other school districts.

During 1977, my life took a change. I got a divorce. I decided to change school districts. I substituted at Greenville High School. I was to work at Benoit High School in Benoit, Mississippi, and this was my first special education assignment. The Benoit school system was the first experience of some white crimes described.

Later, we decided in 1979, or a trial period of marriage to a former husband, to move to Baytown, Texas, in September. My first teaching assignment was for the Houston Independent School District in December 1979, after a brief teaching job at the Baytown Opportunity Center.

Houston Independent School District Principal, Elwood Piper hired me to teach special education classes at John F. Kennedy High School for that spring semester of 1980. The school was a year for high school, and it became an elementary school. I commuted from Baytown to Houston every day for four years.

The special education facilitator allowed me to work on a permit, and I used a deficiency plan to complete twelve hours in learning disabilities. I decided to attend Clear Lake University of Houston that summer in 1980.

The fall assignment took me to another high school, Waltrip High School. While there, I taught secondary resource language arts for students with learning disabilities. I worked there for three years or until 1982. I was to take a year leave, and then I substituted for the Goose Creek

Independent School District for a year. In addition, while on this leave I worked briefly for the Crosby Independent School District in special education.

In 1984, I applied to work for the Channelview Independent School District and I was accepted. Again, I was to teach special education resource language arts for grades nine through twelve. While there for seventeen years, I taught history and math, too. The district built a new high school, and it was high-tech.

There I decided to certify as an assistant principal in 2002. Later, I completed a master's degree in educational administration. In the meantime, I had moved to Austin, Texas, and worked for the Austin Independent School District for about two years teaching special education.

After a brief period, I worked for the Greenwood Public School system for one year in 2004 and 2005. Then, I moved to Houston, Texas, and I am spending time substituting, as well as working on a Ph. D. in Higher Education at Walden University.

Chapter 4
MARRIAGE AND FAMILY

In the summer of July 1967, I was married after working for one year. In the meantime, I continued to live at a boarding house in Glen Allen. It was with co-workers, and my sister had finished college, where she worked and lived as well.

My husband and I moved the following summer to Greenville, Mississippi. We commuted and worked at Glen Allen High School. He became the football coach, and he taught social studies. We started a family in 1969. I gave birth to a son. Then, in 1972, we had a daughter together, and we moved into a new home.

During this period, a co-worker approached me about going back to school. Her name was Dolly Hodges, and she applied for me to attend Mississippi College. There I completed the master's program in social science. My time was spent with working, family and going back to school. I lived on campus one semester, and my husband kept our son, the only child at that time. In addition, I lived in Jackson while studying and completing the program. My daughter was born in the last semester of my study at Mississippi College.

While we worked, babysitters and a nursery kept the children. Their education started in kindergarten at Lakeside Public Schools in Arkansas. My son was an elementary education student in the Greenville Public Schools, and they finished public education in the Goose Creek Independent School District, Baytown, Texas. My son attended the local community colleges. Later, he moved to Austin, Texas, and studied at one of the community colleges. My daughter studied at the Houston universities, and she graduated with a degree in early childhood. Finally, my husband and I remarried in Texas, but later divorced in 1999. We have two grandchildren, and my daughter was married, but later her husband was killed in Houston. Our son is a bachelor and still lives in Austin.

Chapter 5
LIFE IN TEXAS

We moved to Baytown, Texas, in September 1979, and rented a three-bedroom apartment for a half of year. In 1980, we purchased a home in an integrated neighborhood and quiet community. Our children went to a nearby elementary school by bus. It was interesting to meet new faces in a diverse community. The experiences are described to show feelings of race relations, though some isolated, but a concern.

When we left Greenville, Mississippi, a racial group of whites continued harassment, intimidation and threats against me. It started in Greenville, and they continued this saga in Texas. This bias has continued since the 1970s. They use microphones to stir up controversy in the family. It consists of constant abusive language toward me in my home, work place, stores, and other public places. They will go to any means to be heard. For example, I have moved to several apartment complexes, and they have moved into each of them. At my workplace, this group puts smells in the environment. They have a way of letting odor into the school where I work causing stir and animosity. Then, I am blamed or such racism as though the odor is mine.

My family and I disagree on how to deal with their slavery tactics. They believe in medication, thereby staying drugged by psychiatry. This is one-way out I do not stay drugged. I have a life of ambition to work and to stay active. This racist group is annoying, but my family does not know how it feels to know to deal with it. I keep myself very busy by working, family involvement, vacations, singing, and other activities. Instead, when others see it, appropriate force is used. When force is used, other racist whites in hospitals and the use of force handle me by racist police departments. I am very jubilant living alone and much happier.

Finally, this has gotten into my credentials at the state level, but I am determined to prove my innocence. The motive is jealousy. I have documented evidence with the local law enforcement agencies, both state, and federal. The communities have been alerted of this activity.

The fall of 2006, this stalking continued with white people day and night passing a smell like exterminating. It is around 3:00 a. m. in the morning of December 12, 2006, and this woman is calling out, "You ain't going to live with Kareda and Arcell, Jr., " after poisoning. White men and woman are calling out; "You are going to sell dope. You better sell dope or you ain't going to live. You ain't going to live with your family."

In addition, they continue to talk next to my bedroom at night, and they follow me everywhere, including to every job or work. One white woman keeps up everywhere, always near me saying, "Sorry." She is keeping up with the poisoning into my bed; somehow, it is sprinkled and comes over me. She seems to be the main perpetrator and hollering, "You are going to do what I say or you ain't going to live. You are going to sew for me. You can't teach school no way, you are not qualified."

This group follows me through my apartment saying, "You better go back to Mississippi or you ain't going to live." She wants my online schoolwork to use for teaching and says, "You been teaching long enough." She wants to do my online classroom work, and she wants it typed as if she wants it for use. She wants me to take medication, and she brags, put all of them, the whole family, in drugs, and put them in a hospital. She wants to sue me for what has been done by her since the 1970s.

She brags she will make the family move off the land and put them in a mental institution, then sue these states. "These states are in it, too, because they let me go on with it. She blames the entire country for letting her travel over the United States and the Caribbean. A group of white men with her says, "You ought to live with her then." They agree and help her with it. It seems to be one man who helps her get near me. It seems to be one man that gets her in the attic or underneath the flooring because I am on the third floor.

Every time I move, they move in and live around me from room to room, and follow me in my vehicle everywhere. They keep up by talking and observing, every second. This group was using microphones and poison or talking. They have a way of knowing or observing and laughing, showing off how to "kill a nigger."

"You, Jr., and Kareda should go North and live, North to live with us. You better live with your family in Mississippi. You don't need to be working; you better do what they say. You've always done what you wanted, shopped, wore suits, had small feet, and wore blouses to work with white men. You were with those white men, eating on them (oral sex). You did eat on those white men and you better live with us and eat on us, me, too. You are dead, too." When they think we are going to be together, they want to hurry to get rid of me. She proclaims, "You don't need those children." My son called, and they are furious and continuously say, "Sell dope, that was you in Greenville, Mississippi." "You are going to stay on those pills, too." Also, they are near, with a form of sexual abuse or rape, stated, "You are going to feel this and live like this." "I ain't going out of this until you do what I say," they say with group agreement. Some of them seem to tell her to leave it alone, but "you better live with some of these white folks, you're broke anyway." Some says, "I was trying to tell her to come with me." "Money is what I was trying to get." One person proclaims, "I was the one that left it in there and I did not try to get it out of there." The microphones off in the streets, stores, churches, cars, schools, state-to-state, or city to city, or country to country, or airline to airline, with sex, molestation and rape. The bathroom had dripping water over the face bowl in every apartment while I was washing my face. There was form of poisoning in the schools, my truck and other buildings or public places to stop me from working. Others sell the toxics with dismay. They are sex offenders, racists, and threatening. They are trained to commit crimes.

My study is filled with toxicity while doing class work or activity. My telephones are placed publicly at all can hear my conversations. It is an around-the-clock visual, spreading poison during meals. The bathroom smells with tampering. They have continued with bad odors from a body that smelled, such as their feet or sex odors. She accuses me of the smell that I did and do smell, even while working in these schools. They keep it up to prevent us from having money and trying to stop us from getting schooling and good paying jobs. They did not want my children to get an education.

This treatment is the stages of racism from generation to generation of whites. They are using high tech to keep this form of living. This woman has bragged that this will always be my livelihood. My jobs are for motives and hatred. In my last job in Austin, Texas, I was placed on administrative leave with written false reports, and then asked not to come back. My lawyer refused to help with keeping the job. During this period, my gun was confiscated in 2002 in Houston, Texas.

This racist group is waiting with anger to punish because I am not living, as they want me to live. They are always exclaiming, "I was not with my father." They blame others for their actions. I have observed one white male bass voice of distinction that impounded reaction. He is a huge man who comes and goes. I have observed him in Mississippi, but I do not think I saw him. This observation is a feeling of the most high tech white man, but I believe there are two huge white persons with different smells. There is one with an observance that differ with reaction. They have witnessed that parking takes place the opposite of my location within the vicinity. This atmosphere seems to be radar detected with high tech. The power with telephones, race and using vehicles are the main source of the operation. The strategy is to control by poison, and punish for being uncooperative. The emphasis is to sell drugs, sex or prostitution for money and fame with laughter. The act-spilled racism and witnessed generations of whites with pride of color. They spread propaganda to blame others, especially, but ways to capture the audience's attention to control political and economic forces to remain segregated. This class did not transit during integration and desegregation.

The probability is treason with crimes against the government for the 1960s transition of race. This under cover operation is not distinct and is widely publicized throughout the world. This cover is very unacceptable. This racist white group continues to move within my vicinity threatening, shouting and bragging. Threatening means hospitalization tactics; I will be beaten and drugged. They continue to threaten with hospitalization to sell drugs, and this means hard-core drugs. This operation is trying to harass involved with criminal activities. They use microphones to spread personal business about family and myself in public. This entails group activity to prevent me from working as a schoolteacher. Instead, I work as a slave.

As mentioned, these insults are day and night, "If you do not do as I say, then you want get out of this, never." They shout, "You dead, you dead, too." "You better do as these white women want you to," said the white men of the group. They know the craft of sexual assault to forcefully make this operation work. The poison, sexual assault and verbal abuse to force me to do what they want and with these white women. There is a younger girl that helps get what they wanted with giggling and threats. There are signs of using my children to make them unwanted and making them live with their daddy. They are not to visit, and their intention is to make me visible for this white group.

Other instance, this white environment was wiring around my private home, work, car or SUV. Stalking is with racist control without regard for blacks and others. Ventilation vents are filled with fumes by punching an opening in the vents that send air to rooms. This was an air conditioning unit inside of apartment that filters the air using my electricity and phones. The telephone has been bugged since integration.

In 2002, Houston, while obtaining a filled drug prescription downtown, a wave hit the cellular receiver to my ear that left a shock of dizziness. An instance of attempted murder as followed throughout the city as these "white racist" shouted, and reacted as nothing with any conscious. This group hides continuously to promote hatred, out loud and anywhere with no feelings of guilt, just gutless with "I win every time." They can do, go anywhere and do anything because "I am white," just break into places to find me, such as grocery stores, churches, clinics, and the alike. Outright, they talk to others in places about me as singled out.

Another instance, the Wal-Mart and fast food chains and such places are stuffed with their nasty smell. These smells are pointed out to be me. They never have any respect for my children, especially my son suffered and my daughter while job or jobless. They were repeatedly told, "You smell" as I have been constantly treated since the 1970s. Each day they vow for our death. The white woman expressed her desire to kill and surrounded herself by white males who participate. A favorite place to show off very loudly is outside as they hide and sneak around publicly. Neither has the gut to face the public. Instead, they hide in unusual places.

Sadly, they stick around my vehicle, and I am driving using remotes to make the driver's seat move to saturate the bottom or butts of the body. They use different methods to sexually molest, rape and laughing in the public. Then, the "racist" shouts the body stinks and set the schoolroom temperature to sweat to say, "She stinks" or her clothes and arms stinks. Again, they come to every workplace. They find ways to watch me and use the A/C to control the thermostat. The same is done to the school bathroom to experiment and God knows what... They can be heard in the attic and roof of school building or others. They have been listening in on my classroom, since the 1970s. They smell extremely bad like murdered dead in the apartment complex, and they are likened to sex offenders.

This group of people roamed the countryside as though blacks are to blame for their condition or behavior. They spend time begging, stealing, lying and staying in racial controversial confrontations every day. Antichrist or God-hater discussions are favorites to tell me how to act and think white. Clicks are to use brainwashing and propaganda technique strategies to blackmail.

Finally, they are trained to watch every mood as perfected, studying black people. They mimic sayings memorized word for word learned from harassing black people to take control or mind control. There has been constant pressure to control the mind with displeasure of feelings of some sex maniac. They have learned to use ways of finding people off distance inside residents. A type of electricity is used to hear, and machines are used to visualize misconduct publicly. Videos are used to track public grounds or cameras to keep and penetrate victim's private homes or to find us in public places. This "white woman" is out loud proclaiming a family relationship and eager to claim our possession, especially my education. She is sick to control "black people" and their welfare, even to say I am mentally ill. The environment is to kidnap for monetary gains and the white ownership of blacks, since integration.

AFTERMATH

In the wake of this controversy, I have experienced racist attitudes beyond reasonable comprehension because of southern integration, so profound. For example, this group has formed a corporation consisting of controlling plumbing, electricity, cable, telephone, sewage, and any other necessity of life. They maintain this operation by group support. They have a housing unit within my housing unit to hear and keep up with everything. I do not believe they rent, lease, sell or buy. I can smell sewage at all locations, and urine. They have an operation in my transportation, and they are sexual offenders. There is an act of sexual molestation among its women and men.

They are seeking to control southern blacks for their own gain. This group cannot accept blacks as professionals.

Their intention is to control blacks, and to make them slaves. They cannot stand competition, and they have not accepted integration. They are living in the past. Authority does not mean anything to them, and they do not have any self-respect. They feel whites can do anything.

Life has been with corruption that this racist white "stalking" group poisoned the floor area of a computer while typing. My personal mattress has fumes of vicious venom snake poison. This causes sweat to the butt's bottom with the attempt to make Vaginal smell and other body parts. The purpose is to prove racism smell continuously in public since living in Mississippi and Arkansas. A racist tactic is an integration of hate to prohibit my teaching ability. While I was working on the computer, a poison smell evaporated from below. The water supply system is unauthorized at each new location where I live and keep my skin colored. This colors my hand and face with a drip in bathroom face bowl. The new tub was subdued with acid looking coloration that filtered the shower curtain. During work, the group finds me during day in school where their odors smell. The smell causes students to react differently and staff. There is constant racial slur that I smell each day while I work. The microphones are in and around school to help hide and find me. This happens daily work, travel, church and air flights.

This belittling is very descriptive of the slave area with shouting, "You cook and sew for me." One day at a black university, this white woman continued shouting aloud during class getting everybody's attention: "cook and sew." She made it a point that I am from Mississippi and fit only to "cook and sew." I have no need to teach school and be what my daddy wants me to be, although, my daddy sent us to higher educational schools. As mentioned, my father paid for most of my tuition during college days and helped sponsor our nearby college that became a university.

My opinion is that most whites continued to hate integration that school themselves and hated blacks. This group is an example that feared progress and refused to make the transition. They studied ways to intimidate the blacks with fear and a Ku Klux Klan (KKK) tactic to prohibit black educational success. In addition, they describe blacks as ignorant, mentally ill and unfit to teach, instead intimidating them to do household chores. My family was the target to rid the generation with destruction to destroy and my son was so hurt that he lived far away alone. This I knew was happening, but my love for family and humanity as a grave challenge. I refuse to give up or accept, and I continuously worry for my son and daughter grandchildren. We lived this horrible night and day nightmares with God's help to survive. My children were insulted and shunned with fear.

This stalking white group has been monitoring work and following to every substitute job while off a full time job. They group to follow me from home to every destination across the United States. They have a way of lying down to watch undercover in my vehicle while driving or traveling. I can feel their presence and hear loud talking, but continue to drive without fear. A presence feels nothing is taking place. This environment causes different emotions to show mental illness and other kinds of racial destruction to do bodily harm.

This racist tactic is designed to kill and punished, but most likely to hide as using the KKK white sheets. Destructive measures are to subdue the black race and to stop educational progress, especially for my children. This crime was to prevent and hurt me as a black person. I was the target to get rid of because of my stance, and to say "yes sir," "no sir," "yes ma'ma" and "no ma'ma" as an educator. Then the conspiracy was to take the rest of my family and my father's farm. Therefore, these guerillas used underground sewages, bugged telephones and technology to pursue segregation since the 1970s. Some supporters in each state used this torture. Propaganda was certainly distasteful along with other white atrocities. Thus, this experience has a reference to "guerilla warfare."

At each job, most students were saddened and showed remorse, but were cooperative as they tried to continue study. The black population was most helpful with different kinds of observations and support. I did not feel alone because of the hate crimes described for years by race done by some whites. This crime was a KKK characteristic that showed how blacks are treated in the 20th and 21st centuries. There was white jubilation with shouting about how my writing skills were not good enough and how each could win this supposed secret. The laughing and shouting was similar to killing the three (3) Civil Right workers in the 1960s. As you may recall, this group went to a movie, laughed and shouted in the theater, while chewing RED MAN tobacco. When they have achieved certain goals, there is laughing and shouting. Our family was accused of adultery, gossip and confusion with how we smell. Some blacks were to help contain the smell gossip and other ways to pull together segregation as had been with George Wallace and others.

This white game knows how to pull together ways to find me. For example, they scream and shout for attention. The worst encounters are in the morning with filthy smells and surrounded nightly with loud noise. One white woman leads with others pretending "she just wants to leave" and they follow in pursuit with her tactics of sexual hatred. They engage in sex manipulations in secret and public showing off for money or "Show N Tell." She says out loud, "I did it to make money," and presents sex crimes. Their performance is the indulgence of sexual molesters, and sexual offenders. They are a mixture of homosexuals and obesity or outcast groups.

Finally, this cooperation has a way of watching me within my home. They believe the south is going to rise again. I call it the Emmitt Till's syndrome, because they cannot believe blacks should be free. They are disrespectful having no meaningful purpose in life with a seemingly young white girl laughing with immaturity. This young white girl seems to get a thrill joining in sex acts. Nevertheless, they are badly in need of punishment for using our democratic system for selfish means. My feelings are punishment in Alcatraz, San Francisco Bay or Guantanao Bay, Caribbean Sea as the Al Qaeda group for going public national and international. In addition, the death penalty is a need to deter crime like 9/11 and this descriptive agony as tortured.

The radical racist white stalking group has been spraying schools, churches, outdoors and other public places with poison. Again, the bathrooms are a major target with the plumbing and using my job to present bad odors of death. These odors are mostly sex oral odors with bad indecent smells. If I am interested in a job, then they travel daily with bad odors hoping to make me quit and prevent my teaching job. They keep up gossip and loud noise and seek attention to stir up emotions. This obese white male seems to be the key for gaining access to public places with a smart agility with style of "in charge." There seems to be two (2) obese white males that change roles with voice and control. One seems to be working with some form of intelligence as a go between the "Colonels" "Admiral" "Sergeant" who instill how well this thing can perform. They make different sounds like over here or other there to fool authorities or law enforcement.

A cover up role was performed using police devices or transportation. Most of all, they are down-sizing to hiding underground while using technology to gauge electricity and my telephone. The water supply is the main source for poisoning fumes and eventual smells. The telephone has been used since integration to find mail and banks across the United States.

A white woman so-called teacher leader put me in a hospital. While staying in the hospital it happens each time and break-in by this extreme group. She watches over the hospital and attic. I have observed an attack of rape and murder, if possible with threats. A monster attitude to convey what has happened in Greenville, Mississippi, to black girls and men. For instance, a black girl was found murdered in Lake Ferguson, a black girl was murdered with a broom in her Vagina, and a black radio DJ man was murdered during the 1970s. These extreme harsh crimes were witnessed and published.

Other crimes were unsolved, but published with vicious acts of violence that surround my family even today. Therefore, this violence is a continued scare tactic of some Mississippians' whites. There was a hanging in the Kokomo,

Mississippi community with widespread concern within the last decade. Crimes in Texas involved dragging a black man to death in Jasper and the recent "noose" incident in Jena, Louisiana. Another example, the jury, prosecutor, and judge decided six black young high schools (men) were responsible for involving whites hanging a "noose." The group was accused of badly beating a white male student and one black student was sentenced to like twenty years in the Louisiana state penitentiary. Racist groups continually single out blacks since 1619, as though life flowed with racism. Today, the harsh punishment is acts of racism with blacks getting the severest Punishment for crimes.

For instance, my vehicles are set up and used to promote inferiority in all blacks. As a classroom schoolteacher, I am followed with certain technology that is used to intimidate with fear and microphone back and forth in state to state. As mentioned, an international cruise is set up as a tactic; I am white and can go anywhere. Stated, "You should have gone up north," as a particular white woman instills with aggressive behavior. Also, intimidate others by getting rid my son and daughter, stated with arrogant tone with an audience. Out loud, "You being sucking white men" and telling publicly, any place. This is your whipping and you going to "Suck" (orally) sex white men and her. She nags night and day that I must do as she says. I am not going to remarry black men, an outcry of the ignorant.

She seems to be one leader that follows with riding in my vehicle and a loud odor smell as well in the vehicle. They have practiced stringing alone the foul odor, as though it is my odor. It can be smelled in buildings, such as the hallways and alone areas of the rooms or classrooms. One school was targeted with smell from the plumbing in the bathroom, while there the smell was like my bathroom. This act was a demonstration of how I smell using the bathroom and that this insidious behavior to my workplace. Racist behavior is so harsh to stir up smells, and this was how I smelled. As though, I smell working with white people who were stirred up while working in Arkansas and shopping in Mississippi. This racist group has continued such behavior since the 1970s. They hang around places I visit with others' homes and vehicles, with no respect and, outright racism, day and night.

As mentioned, this involves a racist use of a substance to asphyxiate by suffering to death with smells of dust and other foreign fumes. The intake is to damage my internal organs as out loud stated to cause cancer in the body. They engage in any form of contamination to destroy my immune system and brag to each other, "That'll do it, get rid of her, especially her legs. She works all the time and won't be with her men friends like she ought to be, sucking on them." Racist and bragging how to rid my ways of doing things, and won't go with some of these "white men and suck on them," says a rousing white woman, out loud around family and shows no respect. "She went and got her a divorce, instead of sucking on Arcell." They have use racist remarks with attitudes, while listening in on me. My computer is a plaything where they are indulging control with telephone and animosities.

Since a divorce in Texas, they hone in on obscenity, obstruction of justice, and all forms of crimes to show "better do or else." "Better do or else" meant raping family members, and poisoning areas around the computer and television. Also, evaporating poison steam from water into my apartment to intimidate and sexual harass, thus, watching my children and grandchildren to coerce into unlawful activities. "You better take those drugs your family had you taking or else, sell and smoke dope. "You know you being smoking dope." "Your son," all night and day, "your son, ain't with you no more; he'll be selling dope, eating on white women." This has been their topic since the 1970s, "eat on me and eat on these white men." This idiot has been stalking with insulting talk around my children since that time and smarting off in my bathroom and bedroom.

Instances are continued to locate and relocate. They have located me each time, installed personal equipment and walked in buildings or houses with own authority with no respect for personal property. My family's home is the same with this big fat man and woman staging a show looking over their shoulder. The entire family is abused and treated like a pack of animals. "Be with my family, go up north with us or else, be with these ladies, ya'll shop together." One lady usual stated, "You can sew for me," bragging in front of class at Texas Southern University. She brags in the stores, highways, and they giggle on airline flights using racial techniques. As usual, they stink, hollering, "Evelyn" to find me in my private home and walks on heels. They, sound like high heels and use the attic to get to the bedroom. She pretends to be friendly to settle down using body sexual language and a distasteful environment to mold me to do what "I want." "I ain't leaving this alone and I ain't going no where."

This case is saddened instances since the 1970s. As studied, other gang members pretend to beg her to leave, but they all hang around. She shouts at my vehicle in the streets, loudly, to help find other gang members, while traveling in downtown Houston, especially. They hide from law enforcement using my vehicle for cover that is dangerous. Of course, she hides under, around me to survive and is hoping I am murdered. If something happens, "she is not going to live, either." Therefore, my family is used to keeping them alive for their safety and uses our farm for personal safety. The family homes are used in every state like Alabama, Georgia, California and Nevada.

These fanatics are practicing deadly tactics to convey white authority involving hospitals and my job. They have listened in to personal conversations everywhere and with readiness and rudeness twenty four hours day and night. My bedroom is a scene nightly used to convey conservation and somehow to make money. Out loud, this indecent woman shows off a type of sex crime and "I just made me some money" outside my bedroom. She lay around outside my bedroom using poison like the smell of snake venom. Our homes were engulfed with snake and snake sounds before coming to Texas.

Agony continues, "She does not need those children, neither her mother, etc., and she is not qualified to teach school." "She can't read or pronounce words; she just needs to sew for me." "I thought I had gotten her out of that job." "I want her money, to buy what's needed" and they argue, "I wanted her to come with me." "She buys, shops, and dresses them, and I just wanted to take her money and shop. She buys expensive clothing, and can't afford and write checks." "I waiting to send her to jail (man) and take her back to Mississippi to a hospital to stay with her folks." "You shouldn't never have left Mississippi and stayed with your family. That's what your daddy wanted you to do."

In general, some white folks want "upper blacks" to live old slavery ways and refuse to accept blacks, if they are not what they wanted. For example, "She should sing and make money." "I was going to help her make money singing, etc." "She does not need to be with her family and pray like I want her to pray, so I can kill her (during prayer), I want her to say the prayer I want her to pray." I have heard something like it and did not know who it was, neither what happened to such persons.

During moving, I have heard a change in the water and her wading in the underneath the building. I have heard arguments, sounds like sewage covers and heavy equipment around the water supply. The greatest shout was the explosive water movements, on both sides of building and a dead like human or animal smell. This smell has inseminated around living quarters for months. A very loud odor and scents, proclaiming living underneath the floorboard here my family will eventually disappear. "Let junior live and take care of himself" and threatening to bring him underneath. They shout, "Junior, junior, junior" and convey death. These children's grades are not good enough and qualified. "She wants to be a teacher, but her grades and school work is not good enough." "I was trying to make her go back to Mississippi, where she came from. She isn't qualified to teach school in Texas." They travel up and down highways, shouting it out, such as Timeshares in Conroe and Lake Palestine, Texas. Black folks ain't got no business making money and with money.

SUMMARY

This book was to demonstrate some acts of racial injustices experienced since 1619 until today through 2007. I have pointed out several abuse issues of concern to me. The issues are of concern because of illegal questions about my family and me. As I have mentioned, a racist group gang that continues into the millennium. It is sexual harassment, as well.

I am a schoolteacher with more than thirty years of teaching experience in the states of Mississippi, Arkansas, and Texas. I am an African American, but I have referred to myself as a black individual in this book.

This white racist behavior is very depressing, arrogant, and disrespectful. They have no regard for black human life.

They ignore the history of humankind with emphasis on self-motivation. They refuse to take no for an answer. I do not think I should have to compromise my life for someone else's unfortunate situations. They do not respect the laws of the land, and I refuse to be a part of these activities.

I have tried to explain the motive from my point of view. For example, it is a rage of jealousy, racists, money, greed, and self-fulfilling prophecy. I do not know any names, but they know me from teaching school. They are compared to the "skin heads." The major conflict is a group from a class system seeking recognition. They have no respect for minorities, especially some blacks or African Americans. Finally, I am beaten and assaulted daily with their microphones or amplifiers used by talking into places, such as cars, homes, airlines and any other environment. They use toxins to try controlling the victims.

The "white stalking racist" is a professional thief who knows how to "rape" victims. They are professional at stealing using every controlling method that can be possessed to tackle. Trained to follow Africans Americans to use as a scapegoat because they are too lazy to work. Imagine bathing, sleeping, eating, working, traveling and watching television when someone near you smells. They have no regard for blacks' human life.

So typical of "Old Southern" tradition before, during the reconstruction period they used blacks to live. They have not gotten over the transition period of the Civil Rights movement. As usual, blacks are blamed for their mistakes of taking other races for granted. Many southern whites believe it is black people responsibility is to take care of them. The white women are "liars" and use other to help stage the "killing fields." There are "white women" traveling around the United States for attention since the 1970s from somewhere in Mississippi, Arkansas and Texas. In addition, they are begging to treat African Americans special. My life is a showcase for them because being ignorant is commonplace for southern white values. "I am superior."

At my age, they show no respect as though in the 1970s. Neither has come to believe life is the 2000s with technology; rather they live in the 1600s. All energy was focused on being superior and the "white man" game. In this saga, blacks have no life except slavery. These white KKK racists do not believe because being ignorant is no excuse. They are poor, ashamed and never face African Americans who are educated with better jobs. They are "white jobs," and they have not accepted integration or desegregation. I am treated with mental retardation and black, although, I am a three-time college graduate.

This case is similar to the Florida accusations and allegations of a white woman against a black. This group hangs around night and day with ways of rape. They climb in the attic to poison, thereby, using a substance to keep the ventilation circulated with toxins. They can use toxins on my job, trucks and water supply in my environment to convey racism. I have accused "white men" since the 1970s. They have traveled inside and outside the United States.

During 2003, I was to return to Mississippi and forced into a hospital where the group broke into both facilities. They live within the hospitals whenever or wherever and constantly harass me. This group makes up reasons to hospitalize and stay around me to keep me hospitalized by lying. There is one white woman that hangs around me all the time within reach riding under my vehicle or near me within my vehicle. They can use equipment that follows me while driving and they hold conservations. These conservations are to keep within reach and in touch with me. Threats, harassment, intimidations are daily routines.

My telephone is controlled and conservations heard for miles, even my cellular phone. This applies to all telephone communications. We refer to it as "Junk Yard Trash" and any store is their convenience. No Civil Rights exist for this African American woman, and they are adamantly thrilled to celebrate victory. An example is the celebration of the three civil rights workers killed in Philadelphia, Mississippi, and the groups celebrated as shown in the movie, "Mississippi Burning," chewing "Red Man" tobacco while loudly laughing with joy.

As stated, this racist, group uses technology to watch from a distance into any homes, cars, businesses and churches. They know the mail system, and my mail is read before reaching its destinations. My computer was used to provide contact about confidential information. There exists no confidential environment within my vicinity, and everything is exposed about me. I have worked one full school year since 2002, which was in Greenwood, Mississippi. Previously, I moved to Austin, Texas, and they treated me as a helpless victim that ended my job in the Austin Independent School District.

Since that time, I have been a substitute teacher. I have been often threatened at work, and they live where I work with a bad smell and used to accuse me of smelling. This is their racist endeavor and motives. In addition, as a schoolteacher, this group has made it known that I am not a competent employer. As an African American, I am unfit to be a schoolteacher. I, instead I need to sew for her or be a house cleaner.

Late nights were used inquiring and programming information from my home. I am awaken by loud sounds of microphones coming from my bedroom, bathroom and over the television or radio sounds. This is calls for medication, promotions by the group and rally around everyone to set up hospitalized for medications.

After moving to Houston, Texas, in the summer 2005, there was ascension of hatred using microphones melting in the street that continued to sun down. This act is a thrill to them that continues to flow. I do not know how many, but they have a way of conning entailing rape, gossip and lies. They spent the summer 2006 and going into winter with the same activities. They are loud with toxic, noise pollution and store hatred. I am the one who is mentally retarded and need medication that is their program, do as I say. Racist claims that I am the problem and I should move back to my folks in Mississippi. I need to pick cotton and work in the fields; I am unfit to be a schoolteacher.

Presently, while working on a Ph.D. that "I am not qualified" and the women keeps the public informed on progress. The negative report card is one particular way a white woman of the group portray competency with her racist gang. As I moved down the street, they moved into the same building and they are living around me. The bathroom, bedroom, bed, and the ventilation are set for their thrilling environment. If the environment is not a good enough death trap, then other odors are poured into my apartment night and day.

The family resident is same environment with these white aggressive "overseers" involving threats, blackmail and a sense of ownership. There is constant fear riding, indoor, and traveling by airline or at the airport. Constant finger pointing, the black intimidating environment has been the scene of such behavior since the 1970s.

Today, we are experiencing hatred in schools, such as the "noose" on campus and riding of students in the back of the school bus. For instance, this white group lives in the attics and floorboards to harass night and day. They change the water plumbing with tactics to make my bathroom smell and remove the chlorine or no chlorine smell. Each time the move is violent and a loud odor as a smell of death. The feel of murder is among them with the arguments. There is crying out of arguing among them with such shouts as "don't do that." They have shouting ways to find me anywhere like home, work, shopping, traveling, etc., with such voice to manipulate and racist control. Their odors are horrible smells and disease threatening.

Basically, there have been contacts made to authorities, such as local, state and federal with no avail to stop or prevent in public places such as libraries, post offices, courthouses and air travels. It seems to be a sense of pride to live before or remain segregated, instead of making transitions under federal statures to comply with presidential, congressional and judicial orders. They are tied to the "Old South" with the former Alabama Governor, George Wallace personification theory of black people. A sense of vow is to live with likeness of the Ku Klux Klan with constant threat of violence and intimidation and lies. Their smell is sexual raping with ways to harm others with rape and practiced openly in the public. This indecent exposure is done in the presence of the young and old with no respect, anywhere, living like a beast or animal. Further, this group is young and older whites that hide constantly to keep from facing justice.

My reports have been sent to the Houston Police Chief, but protocol exceeds human dignity. Reports were sent to some of the House and Senate members without group capture for these crimes. The agony is privacy in the home and disrespect to my family. As to privacy, while taking the state tests, such as the TECAT and the Principal certification, this group was intact around me the entire hours. The GRE and law school entrance tests involved loud noise of giggling, insults and tested in an enclosed booth area. This racist group has spent days of insane behavior in my classroom with my own audience with such likeness. They are found at my job or every corner to insult and practice superiority. *BELIEVE ME OR NOT! ASK WHAT HAPPENED TO BLACK HANGINGS! MURDER OF BLACKS WITH KANGAROO COURTS! DR. REV. MR. MARTIN LUTHER KING'S MURDER! THE MISSISSIPPI DAM MURDERS OF THREE CIVIL RIGHTS WORKERS CALLED "THE MISSISSIPPI BURNING"*

MOVIE! MANY, MANY, MANY, OTHERS, WE DO NOT HAVE A RECORD! LOST OF LIFE TO RACISM!

AS TO HOSPITALS, BE AWARE OF RACIST WHITE MOODS AND INTENTION TO RAPE AND MURDER SETUPS.... THIS ENTIRE SAGA IS RACISM AND I AM IN CONTROL WITH GOD'S HELP OF MY OWN LIFE. FAMILY THREATS ARE A MAJOR CONCERN THAT INTENTION A REALITY TO MURDER ALL FAMILY MEMBERS, ESPECIALLY MY SON AND DAUGHTER. THEY HAVE FOUND WAYS TO SET THEMSELVES ON FAMILY PROPERTY IN MISSISSIPPI AND MY INTERMEDIATE FAMILY PROPERTY.

HOW BOLD! I AM GOING TO FIGHT WITH GRACE AND NO DISMAY WITH GOD'S HELP! IN ADDITION, PRAYERS! THEY ARE NOT INTELLIGENT TO COURT FIGHT, BUT LOVE OLD WAYS OF SLAVERY. THE DRED SCOTT CASE, CIVIL WAR AMENDMENTS, CIVIL RIGHT ACTS, NOR THE VOTING RIGHT ACTS ARE RESPECTED. THE COURT HOUSE IS TREATED LIKE "WHITE SUPERMACY" FAIRY TALE. I WAS CALLED TO JURY DUTY WITH NO RESPECT, FOLLOWED THROUGH THE COURTHOUSE AND I DECIDED TO

LEAVE ON ONE OCCASION WITH RESPECT FOR THE ACCUSED UNTIL PROVEN INNOCENT OR GUILTY. I DID NOT PARTICIPATE WITH REGARD FOR CITIZEN INDIVIDUAL RIGHTS "DUE PROCESS" AND THE FOURTEENTH AMENDMENT.

DO YOU THINK "HATE WHITE GROUPS" RESPECT BLACK PEOPLE EDUCATION, WITH NO REGARD FOR HUMAN DIGNITY AND BLACKS TREATED AS INFERIOR? HOWEVER, LIFE GOES ON WITH GOD'S PLAN AND RACISM IS PLAIN IGNORANT WITH STUPIDITY. WE ARE GOING ON WITH OUR SOUTHERN JOBS, INSTEAD OF RUNNING NORTH BECAUSE INTEGRATION REMAINS FOREVER, EVERYWHERE.

"Walking on Water"

Lots of people feel free
Walking on water means they must feel free and
close to thee
If I only could see what it means to thee;
Then walking on water would mean you are free
Gon ahead and walk close to thee
Finally, we all will be free.

By Evelyn White

To many Niggas & hoes, be trying
To take me off of my game.
They see me balling, so they
Wanta take me off my chain.

By Arcell Jacob, Jr.

APPENDIX

INDEX